The Christian in a Changing World

Monasticism and the New Realities of Life

Archimandrite Vasileios

Abbot of Iveron Monastery, Mount Athos

Translated from the Greek by

Dr. Elizabeth Theokritoff

Alexander Press

Montréal, Québec, Canada

BY THE SAME AUTHOR

Beauty and Hesychia in Athonite Life
Europe and the Holy Mountain
Ecology and Monasticism
Monastic Life as True Marriage
Abba Isaac the Syrian
The Saint: Archetype of Orthodoxy
The Meaning of Typikon
The Parable of the Prodigal Son
Hymn of Entry (SVS Press)

The Christian in a Changing World

2875 Douglas Avenue
Montréal, Québec
H3R 2C7 CANADA
Tel: (514) 738 5517
Fax: (514) 738 4718

ISBN: 1-896800-12-2

The Christian in a Changing World

Monasticism and the New Realities of Life

Series: "Mount Athos"
Number Seven

Cover: Double-headed Byzantine eagle, atop a small wall fountain. Inside the main entrance of Iveron Monastery, Mount Athos
Courtesy of Douglas Lyttle ©

Editor's Note

As editor of Alexander Press, it gives me great joy to continue the series "Mount Athos" with the publication of five more essays by Archimandrite Vasileios, Abbot of Iveron Monastery on Mount Athos, almost one year since the warm reception of the first four volumes of this series. These five newly translated texts will be published in separate volumes and one of them includes additional material by Professor Georgios Mantzaridis.

Fr. Vasileios (Gondikakis), born on Crete in 1936, studied theology in Athens and in Lyon, France. After visiting Mount Athos, he felt "at home," and decided to remain there. Initially he stayed in a hermitage close to the Elder Paisios. In 1968, he was asked to become the abbot of the Stavronikita Monastery. In his twenty-two years (1968-1990) as abbot, a life-giving breeze of renewal and a particular intensity of stillness and watchfulness *(hesychia and nepsis)* which characterize Athonite spirituality, has been treasured by thousands of visitors and pilgrims who through their personal experience in a very simple and humble way "taste and see that the Lord is good."

In 1990 Fr. Vasileios assumed the leadership of the Iveron Monastery, becoming its abbot and reintroducing its cenobitic life.

Fr. Vasileios was first introduced to the English-speaking public through his well known work *Hymn of Entry* (SVS Press: "Contemporary Greek Theologians") in which he was described by Bishop Kallistos (Ware) as the pioneer of the striking revival and renewal of monastic life on the Holy Mountain whose message was "a word of life not for Athos only but for the Christian world as a whole."

Over the last twenty-nine years, Fr. Vasileios has spread this message beyond the borders of Mt. Athos by participating in, and speaking at, theological meetings, youth conferences, and gatherings of the faithful. The present series of "essays" (in reality, speeches edited for publication) is an attempt to bring the English-speaking public more of the "fresh vision of theology, Church, and the world" offered by the Holy Mountain through the original yet genuinely traditional voice of Fr. Vasileios.

The seventh text of the series entitled "The Christian in a Changing World" was the talk delivered by Fr. Vasileios and the subsequent discussion at the Fourth Orthodox Youth Conference at Panagia Soumela Monastery Verroia, Greece on July 17-22, 1989. The conference was organized by the Youth Education Group of Syros (Neanikos Epimorphotikos Omilos Syrou) and the proceedings published by them in Greek in 1992.

The translation — adaptation from the Greek text was done by Dr. Elizabeth Theokritoff.

The series "Mount Athos" will be continued, God-willing, with other Athonite texts and monographs to be published in 1998.

Dr. John Hadjinicolaou
Dormition, 1997

THE CHRISTIAN IN A CHANGING WORLD

Monasticism and the New Realities of Life

I think we should thank the Church: the Lord, the Mother of God, the Saints, the Holy Spirit who "holds together the whole institution of the Church" and gives strength to the humble, the quiet and the insignificant. Because what we have experienced here* is a blessing, a blessing that is given to the quiet and the humble. What is happening here is something that amazes and delights because it is simple, and it is organised by a little group on a Greek island. It is not organised from Athens or Thessaloniki or any other major centre. It is organised by a little group which has at its head a simple and humble man who is known to all of us. So the whole atmosphere here already brings us more tangibly into the Church, and brings us into monasticism. Now, all the rest that has happened appeals to me because it has been monastic and quiet — that is, because it has been confused and unquiet. I believe there are two languages, two ways of dealing

* Fourth Orthodox Youth Conference on the Theme of "Youth in a Changing World" at Panagia Soumela Monastery, Verroia, Greece on July 17-22, 1989, organized by the Youth Education Group of Syros. (Neanikos Epimorphotikos Omilos Syrou)

with things. One is the Orthodox way, the Orthodox language which is man's mother tongue. The other way is mechanical, created, artificial; it is an irrational way which appears in the guise of logic, just as the devil often appears in the guise of an angel or of Christ; and this method of approach dazzles without shedding light. I believe that all that has happened and all that has been said here during these days manifests these two forces: on the one hand Christ and the light of Christ which "illumines all", and on the other that other light which dazzles without shedding light.

The general title of our theme, if I remember rightly, is "The Christian in a changing world". This is a title that is real and alive. The title assigned to my own talk is "Monasticism and the new realities of life". Let me tell you how I could deal with this topic in a logical way. I could talk about monasticism while at the same time betraying monasticism and being a pain to you. And you would say, Can't you just leave us alone! Monasticism and the new realities of life. There are new realities in our life, and now we live in such and such a way. The other day at the monastery we had a bore-hole put in, 100 metres deep, with an air balloon device worked by such and such a machine so that we can get water up, whereas before we used to get water from the spring. Before, we used to keep the fish in the monastery cellar where it was cool; now we keep it in the deep freeze. So what? Another thing: they say that monks ought to go out into the world. Or that they ought to get an education, and help, and provide for the needs of the community. And I think of a Western monastery, or indeed many Western monasteries, which have areas of specialisation, and they say that this monastery does this kind of work, and that one does something else. So the monks of this monastery are teachers; they are educated men, they have doctorates, they organise conferences, they write books and are better at communicating with teachers and people who are well up in contemporary literature. Others are simpler people. But this is in a certain way a betrayal of monasticism. And when something betrays monasticism in the Orthodox Church, it betrays man.

Monasticism is valued here because it is not monasticism, "aloneness";[1] because it is a catholic existence. And the significance of the monk is that he is not alone, he is with everyone else. As I have said before in connection with love and marriage, the monk is one who is "married"[2] So when someone asks you: Why did you go and become a monk? You say, I don't know. Can you explain why the flower turns towards the light? It does it in order to live. How can you answer the question: Why did you become a human being? Why do you breathe? It just happened; that's the way it is.

---

[1] Monachos, "a monk", literally means "one who is on his own". This play on words should be borne in mind wherever the author speaks of "monk" and "non-monk".

[2] Cf. Archimandrite Vasileios, *Monastic Life as True Marriage* . (Montreal, Alexander Press, 1996).

And the answer to the question: Why did you become a monk? is: It just happened. Each person went to the monastery for a different reason. But all the reasons resolve themselves into one sole reason: that God loves us all, and calls each of His sheep by its own name and sets it apart. So you start talking about the Holy Mountain without knowing why you went there. Something drew you there. And now what do you find? First of all, you see that whatever is said about monasticism, whatever conception of it is formed from the outside, has nothing to do with what attracts and draws you. (Let me say parenthetically — I am not delivering a talk. I just want to provide some starting points for discussion.) First of all, you notice: I feel at home here. They speak a different language here. I find everyone here. Something was said earlier about the struggle between the generations, the generation gap separating young and old. Another phrase we have heard is, "We don't trust the young". But in monasticism, on the Holy Mountain, everything is turned upside down. Everything appears differently; everything is free. And I should like to say about the struggle between generations — there isn't one. There is no old and young. Someone only a few years old is not young, because in that case man would be ill-fated and tormented because he would be condemned to grow old. And someone many years old is not old, because then we are up against the same problem for man. And one who has fallen asleep is not dead. But ultimately, it is the real person who is young. And the real person is one who has found himself. The one who has found himself is one who loses himself. And you truly find what you lose. Whoever loses his soul for another then finds his soul. He finds the other. In other words, he finds everyone. So each person sums up the Church, so we find ourselves in a different realm, a different logic, a different state.

I may be a monk; I may wear a monastic cap. But that means nothing. I may have a beard, and for that matter a white one...

A monk was once asked: How long have you been on the Holy Mountain? He answered, "The jackals have been on the Holy Mountain along time, but they're still jackals." Another thing that has been said is that you should go out to meet others. St. Anthony, too, says that our salvation lies in others. If we save and gain our brother, then we have gained God; and when we scandalise our brother, then we have lost God. The struggle between generations, young and old, married and single. These things are all relative. Man is not satisfied with the liveliness of youth. Man is not satisfied with the good sense of old age. Man is not satisfied with the shattering experience of love and what it can give him, belonging as it does to a physical or psychological realm where everything turns out to be a wild goose chase. I am looking for something else. And that something else exists. And when you find it, then everything else — everything created, transient, inferior — is given to you in a different way. It is clothed in a different light. And then what is mortal is swallowed up in immortality; what is corruptible, in incorruption; and we live in the flesh as if we were living in heaven. The struggle between the generations. The young are restless and want new ideas, revolutions, new people. The young to me are people who want something real, that is, they want something of great stillness. Stillness, *hesychia,* is a tremendous revolution which has ended in stillness, in calm, in non-revolution and in play. The young, the dear, the ever-living one who has a place in our heart and will be with us even in the grave, is the one who dissolves his own self and lives for the other. The others are his life. And he does this in such a way that he feels it was not his own action; it was a gift that was given him. And he does not boast of it. If he starts to boast, that means it is false, and he has lost it. This humble man has received an embrace from Christ, from God, and has himself become god by grace, and wants to be dissolved, to empty himself, to cease to exist in order that the other may exist.

A great fuss is being made at the moment about Kazantzakis and *"The Last Temptation of Christ"*. Some say that Kazantzakis is a demon, others that he is a restless spirit, others again that he is a theologian or a Church Father. So what is he? I'll tell you what he is: a wretched creature, a human being. That makes him sympathetic. It has been said that we are all obliged to Kazantzakis for something: the merciless application to his work that he imposed on himself, without asking any recompense from anyone. This is true, and it is something moving. And when you approach him, you have a sense that he is like a wild, inaccessible Cretan mountain. But you can't warm to the poor man, because he was searching for himself. A simple man, a sailor, once told me: I was reading one of Kazantzakis' books; I wasn't a religious man. At one point I got annoyed with it and threw it into the sea. You read him, you say, all right, he worked hard; but you don't warm to him. I would not compare him with a saint. I am not going to talk to you about Abba Isaac. I am going to talk about Dostoevsky. Dostoevsky is regarded as someone who dissects the soul. He is not a great novelist who dissects the soul. What is he? He is a tormented orthodox. He has understood the secret. He happens to have a gift for writing. He writes novels, and while the reader thinks he is reading a novel, Dostoevsky implants in him the "germ" of Orthodoxy, so to speak. A secret consolation. You warm to Dostoevsky, because with his whole being he gives a commentary on Abba Isaac the Syrian. Everyone warms to Dostoevsky, believers and atheists and people who won't speak to each other. Why? Because Dostoevsky is humble. It is what I said before, that the monk is a non-monk, one who is not on his own. The monk, ultimately, is a revelation of man. He is a man who has gone "outside the camp", (Hebrews 13:13) called by God even though he did not deserve it, and because that was the will of God, Who does whatever He wills. But if it happens that this man who is called becomes a monk and dissolves, in other words does not live for himself, then this is a blessing for everyone. We were saying a few days ago that man gives off a radiation. It was also said that the soul of each person is worth more than the whole world. And this is not something theoretical, but something we can touch. If we had spiritual senses, if we could just become wholly sensitivity, then we should see that the old man who has the grace of God is young. He is ever-living and always contemporary. Someone who creates a "revolution" is simply making a noise. A preacher who takes it upon himself to teach is often nothing more than a machine generating noise pollution. A holy, humble man who does not speak spreads a calm which consoles our inmost parts. Another humble man who sits and talks to himself, is talking to everyone. Dostoevsky soliloquises through all his heroes, and each person finds true consolation. While someone else who sets himself up as a teacher and wants to teach everyone in a mechanical way, just drives people away. A humble man offers himself as rich compost to nourish the roots of the other's being, and he himself draws all the others to himself. Abba Isaac says that the more the humble man flees from the world, the more people pursue him and want to be with him. The egotist, the person who boasts about himself and disparages others, repels people; he lives in solitude, and lives in hell. So it is the non-monk who is in solitude.

The first time I went to the Holy Mountain, I had the sense that something is going on here. Afterwards, people outside asked me, "Tell us something about the Holy Mountain, since you went there and liked it". But, I told them, I can't say anything. Because it was like pulling at a thread, as they say, and the whole quilt comes up; and then you realise you can't lift the whole thing. You can't express the inexpressible. But one day the answer came. I found the passage in the Philokalia where it says, "A monk is one who is separated from all and united with all."[3] So I said, right, that's what it is. He has separated himself from everything and united himself with everything. Since he has been given a gift and because it was given to him, and is a gift of God, it does not belong to him; it belongs to everyone. So ultimately, as we have said, the monk is man —man in his catholicity, in a universal sense. We said before that the youth can be an old man. You know, one can be born old. And the Apostle Paul could never grow old. And at the same time we said that when you talk about a monk, you are talking about man, and you find the grace of the monk among people who are humble; and I talked about Dostoevsky. I can go on to say something more daring: you can approach someone who is not in the Church, and who is yet an image of God, an actual human being, someone who does not want to torment others. And you are moved, and feel that here is a brother of mine, some-

[3]. Evagrius of Pontus, On Prayer 124, *Philokalia* Vol. I, tr. Palmer, Sherrard and Ware (London, Faber & Faber 1979), p. 69.

body I can sit down with. Whereas you may see a monk and say: I can't sit next to this man. This is not my decision. It is decided by other powers which I have no control over. I would run a mile from such a monk.

I want to go back to the first sort of person. I will mention Kafka. He was a Jew, of course, not even a Christian. I think that a child reading his writings might be disappointed; but what he writes is the discharge from his suffering. And inasmuch as he is genuine, he reveals something of the monk, he reveals something of the Orthodox human being. As a pine tree exudes resin and a mastic bush mastic, so he exudes his pain. And his writing gives shape to his pain, and that makes it something human and true. He says, I felt my father was a boot that trod on me, and I was the worm that was trodden underfoot. And when I wrote, it was as if the worm stuck its head out and moved it about a bit. Writing was not a release. Writing was something of a consolation. People said he should help others. He replied, Who am I to help others when I can't help myself? Rilke said that Kafka wrote the best German prose of all. And Kafka lived in Prague with Rilke and never saw Rilke. He was not interested in German prose, he was interested in the pain erupting from his heart. In this man, formed in the image of God, this non-Orthodox, who suffers pain, you sense something monastic, something Orthodox. This is why I want to say that when you go to the Holy Mountain you feel that here I am not in a club, I am not in a party, I am not attached to a point of view, I am not attached to an ideology or whatever. I am at home, a home which is a warm nest for the whole world, and at the same time wider than the heavens. You hear a clear voice spoken in silence. A grace which brings everyone together and a blessing which gives each person the possibility of finding himself, finding the rhythm of his life, hearing his name and speaking his own language. And those who are separated are brought together in fellowship, the dead come to life, those yet to be born are present, because the Spirit who has neither beginning nor end is always in charge of each and all, and each person is everyone.

A man once came to the Holy Mountain and wanted to make fun of the monks. He went to a hut where there was an old man who used to whisper the prayer: "Lord Jesus Christ, have mercy on me a sinner." The man asked him, "Why do you say 'Have mercy on me a sinner,' instead of praying for the whole world?" Unperturbed, the old man replied, "We are all one." When a monk says the prayer, he says it for everyone. And his life is an offering to the whole world. And his existence is a fulfilment of the Lord's prophecy which says that "I have other sheep which are not of this fold; I must bring them also, so there shall be one flock, one shepherd." (John 10:16)

Here you do not understand things with your brain. But the whole of your being is dissolved and simplified and becomes, so to speak, an organ of understanding. And the whole person understands in the process of being given totally to God. And at some point God gives man, not a knowledge of transient things, but a grace, that same grace of God which "has brought all things from non-existence into being", a grace which makes man "virtually uncreated and god by grace". And deification, as St. Maximus the Confessor says, has no genesis but "an inconceivable Manifestation." These are the things ineffable and incomprehensible which are not taught, but imparted to man suddenly, unexpectedly. And they are imparted to the person who waits patiently— I would say, who does not hurt others. (This is a minor virtue and of the greatest, not to hurt others. Instead of saying, "I think, therefore I am", I believe we could say, "I forgive, therefore I am"). If then someone patiently endures each trouble which God allows him to experience — and troubles are a blessing — if he forgives everyone and has nothing against anyone; at some point, unexpectedly and without external cause, as Abba Isaac says,[4] the grace of God will come. Then man is illumined, and becomes light by grace.

Then he does not simply know the unknown mystery of the beginning and the end, but he himself comes to be without beginning or end. And remaining there, he remains with everyone.

---

4. Cf. Homily 53, *The Ascetical Homilies of Saint Isaac the Syrian* tr. Holy Transfiguration Monastery, Boston (Boston, 1984), p. 264.

I should like to end by destroying some idols. It is not being "good" that makes a monk, and your aim should not be to become "good." Orthodox monasticism is not "good", just because it has educated monks. Someone was saying to me, "Do you know how many educated monks the Roman Catholics have?"

As an example: we had a monk in the monastery who knew several languages, and we also had an old Romanian monk, Father Bartholomew, who had come to the Holy Mountain at the age of 13, and had been at the monastery for eight years because he had Parkinson's disease. In his last days everyone was very fond of him and would visit him in his cell. Someone said to him, "You know, Father Bartholomew, this foreign monk is highly educated and speaks English, German, French, Russian and Serbian." And you know what this old Athonite monk's reaction was? "Does he speak Gypsy? Well then, he doesn't know anything!"

To the Athonite monk, the point is not how many languages a person speaks. The point is, whether or not he has gone beyond death.

What matters is that we should be Orthodox. But are we or aren't we? In some of the informal conversations we have had with brothers here, I have said, Orthodoxy is the thing, and that's it. So someone says to me, with justification, What do you mean by talking in such absolutes? I grant that objection; you have a point. But I would say to you: The Orthodoxy I am talking about is non-Orthodoxy. And the monasticism is non-monasticism. And God is not one who can be known; He is higher-than-divinity *(hypertheos).*

And Christ is "He who sits on high with the Father and here is invisibly present with us". If He were here visibly, He would not be God; He would be something else. So the whole world stands in need of this spirit: the Roman Catholics and the Protestants and the Buddhists and atheists and believers and people in the year 2000 and whoever else. And Orthodox monasticism says to man in a changing world: The changes are rapid and amazing and, as we have said, insignificant and paltry. This monasticism, as you know, is ever contemporary — that is to say, it is beyond time. And the desert within is what we all long for, the pulsating community of life. And when we talk about ecumenism and about the heterodox, we will have to love them, to shake them up, to wear them out — but wear them out with love. The worst of it is that we do not have the power to do this for them; but God has the power to do it out of love.

How often we go to meetings with Roman Catholics and Protestants, and, ostensibly out of love, we make polite noises. But worldly politeness is a mockery that belongs to the present age. And man does not need mockeries. He needs the grace of God which deifies him, which transcends death. And this is to be found within monasticism; it exists in our tradition. This is why I say that ultimately, it is the new human being who is the true monk. And a person in the world who is humble has an affinity with the true monk; he is not alien to the eternal youth which the Lord bestows.

The point is that we can be baptised into a spirit in which differences are transcended, where we are all united, where we are all free and make up the Church of the firstborn. We are all firstborn, and each of us sums up the Church, sums up the whole in miniature. This is the life, the faith and the gift of Orthodoxy; this is the language it speaks. It says nothing else; it repeats the same thing.

I refer you to some passages of the Philokalia which underline this same truth.[5] Blessed is the monk who regards every man as God, after God. Blessed is the monk who looks with great joy on everyone's salvation and progress as if it were his own. Blessed is the monk who regards himself as the offscouring of all things (I Corinthians 4:13). There was the young monk who said to his elder that "with God's help, I feel that my mind dwells constantly amidst the things of God." And his elder told him that that was nothing great; the great thing is to regard "yourself as lower than all creation."

And the words we have already heard: the monk is one who is separated from all and united with all.

---

5. Evagrius of Pontus, On Prayer 121-125, *Philokalia* Vol. I, tr. Palmer, Sherrard and Ware (London, Faber & Faber 1979), pp. 68-69.

Because he wanted to be united with all things, if he were united with one thing separately, he would then be separated from all the other things which he did not want to leave out. And the miracle happened: he embraced everything, he found room for everything within himself by dint of separating himself from it. This is why I say that there is a withdrawal, a departure, which is in the nature of a return: one flees from society and returns to it.

You go away, and by going away you are led into the communion of all. And there is a descent which leads you up. You descend with humility, you are voluntarily broken, you accept this (if you are found worthy to consider yourself lower than all creation.) And then you experience what we talk about in the service for Theophany, "By going down [into the water] we have ascended to God". And a final quotation: Blessed is the monk "who regards himself as one with every man, through always seeing himself in each of his brothers."

Discussion

Question: You said that we should not become good.

Fr. Vasileios: Do you believe that you are good, or that you are going to become good?

Reply: No.

Fr. Vasileios: Well then, you are in no danger!

Question: What should we become, though?

Fr. Vasileios: Bad! [Applause] You see, I think that becoming good, in the secular sense of good, is a joke. We have got so many troubles — do we need to make jokes of ourselves? If we become Orthodox, I think we are beyond good and evil. Not in Nietzsche's sense, but as the Church experiences it. Here we have Abba Isaac. There are three homilies which speak about three degrees of knowledge.[6] At the first level, he says, you have secular knowledge, fleshly knowledge, the logic that makes people stick stubbornly to their opinions and produce theories, and overturn theories, and use other contrivances. At that point a man thinks that the providence of everything is to be found in this knowledge. Like those who say "There is no governance in these visible

---

[6] Ed. Spetsieris, Numbers 63-65; = *The Ascetical Homilies of St. Isaac the Syrian* (tr. Holy Transfiguration Monastery, Boston 1984), Hom. 52, p. 258f.

things." There is no governance in visible things, so I am organising them. And what happens? This is why this person who is so knowledgeable is possessed by faintheartedness, sorrow and despair, and fear of demons, and trepidation before men and anxiety over illnesses and concern over want and the lack of necessities and the fear of death, the fear of sufferings. Why? Because he does not know how to "cast his care upon God through the confident trust of faith in Him." He does not know how to abandon himself to God. So then what happens? This knowledge examines the small faults of other people and their causes, and their weaknesses, and it arms a man for stubbornly upholding his opinion and for disputation, and aids him in cunningly employing devices and crafty contrivances — and this is the phrase which is important — "and the other means which dishonour a man". It is concerned with the means which dishonour the human being, which degrade his majesty. Whereas Abba Isaac says that "by humility, knowledge of the truth perfects the souls of those who have acquired it." The knowledge of truth is perfected in humility.

The second degree, the second stage involves a struggle of soul and body; it involves fasting, prayer, almsgiving, reading the Holy Scriptures. And the modes of virtue and the struggle with the Passions and the rest. And when one has attained many virtues and many struggles, one's knowledge is composite and corporeal.

And we go to the third stage, where this distraction of secular knowledge does not exist. That carnal and corporeal state of ascetic exercises of body and soul does not exist: the fasting, prayer, almsgiving and reading of the Holy Scriptures. So what does exist? What exists is an awestruck wonder and a rest. In that state, man does nothing. It is done by Him who has neither beginning nor end. Then man understands why the world was created out of non-existence. Why man became man, and what is the meaning of the image of God, and why he is an image of God. What it means that he should begin and go forward in freedom. The meaning of what we were saying: that he speaks personally, he speaks his own language, he finds his own rhythm. And then after that he passes beyond everything and reaches a point where he is relieved even of his own free will. Then "man does not direct himself, but is led by another guidance."[7] Then he finds himself in the captivity which is higher than any freedom. The aim is to reach that point. So we are free when we are prisoners of the grace of the Holy Spirit. And the thing is that man is able to reach that point. All the other great and momentous things we have talked about are the things that dishonour man.

This is the great idea that Orthodoxy has about man. It is not that we should become "good". Abba Isaac says in another place[8] that the Lord commanded His disciples: "Remain in the city of

---

[7] *Ascetical Homilies* 23, p. 119.
[8] *Ascetical Homilies* 77, p. 384.

Jerusalem until you are endued with power, when the Holy Spirit comes. Jerusalem is to be understood as virtue. The power from on high is humility." That is why he says that the grace and the reward are not given for virtue or for the labour of virtue, but for the humility which in engendered by virtue. This power, then, is the Comforter. "This power is the Comforter Himself, who, in the strength of faith, consumes the parts of the soul as if by fire. The soul then... despises every danger because of her trust in God, and on the wings of faith she soars aloft, taking leave of visible creation. She becomes as one drunken in the awestruck wonder of her continual solicitude for God; and by simple, uncompounded vision and by unseeing intuition of the divine nature, she accustoms the intellect to attend to rumination upon its hidden things."[9] He receives this grace, he receives this power and becomes as it were out of his mind, as if drunk, and protected by another power, a power which is never going to leave him. And this power is no threat to anyone. And this power is a blessing for everyone. So that is where Orthodoxy and the Church is leading us, not to the other things which are lies. And let me say something else. If I am good and I boast about my goodness and this goodness and this boasting of mine wounds someone else, what good is this goodness to me or to the other person? I'd do better to be bad.

---

[9] *Ascetical Homilies* 52, p. 263.

Again, I remember Abba Isaac's words where he says that virtue without humility is useless or rather harmful. And humility alone can save man. I myself have seen some "bad" Athonites on the Holy Mountain, and because they were "bad" they were saints, and they reduced me to shreds by the way they behaved.

I went to a monastery once, and there was an old hieromonk there who did not have a good reputation. And when I went there he spontaneously made a prostration before me and said, you honour the *rason,* you honour the Holy Mountain.

Once a fire broke out at Karyes, and we fought it all night; and after our struggle to put out the fire in the forest, we reached a cell. The Elder there gave us water and raki, and before drinking the raki we made the sign of the Cross, saying a prayer. And there was a monk who did not have a good reputation (he had a very bad reputation), and he said, "The Mother of God help us — it's for her that we've come here, after all." This sense, that he feels like a helpless child of the Mother of God — it turns you to pulp. We don't do anything. Christ and the Mother of God do it all. If we understand that, they will raise us up to great heights.

I remember something that St. John Chrysostom says in his homily on the Ascension, commenting on "and we shall be caught up in the clouds" (1 Thessalonians 4:17): The rich man is not fortunate nor the poor unfortunate, but whoever attains to being 'caught up' [is fortunate]". This is why I believe that on the Holy Mountain the thing is to have the sense that you are not good, that you are a mess, a good-for-nothing, an abject creature. But despite all this, there is a scandal: that Christ insists on loving you. And when you realise this, abject creature as you are, you say: shouldn't I do something? And the Mother of God helps you, and you do something good. On your own, you can do nothing.

Question: You said that whoever loses his life for another, that person finds his life. Can you say something more on that?

Fr. Vasileios: But that is in the Gospel, isn't it? "He who loses his life, the same shall save it" (Matthew 10:39)...

Question: But the part about the "other", losing our life for another —always putting the other person first.

Fr. Vasileios: If we do not live for ourselves, but for Him who died and rose again for our sake and for our brothers, then we truly find ourself. Ourself, which is everyone else. Because "we who are many are one body and one spirit." And we say that one who has the grace of God is close to us, one who has the grace of God is young, one who has the grace of God comforts us and helps us and lights the paths of our life here and of the life beyond death. As the Bishop of Chania was saying yesterday, that when he sees a young man and woman going out together he is glad, it is natural; it is good; he just thinks about whether it will end in marriage. And I say, it should end in marriage within the Church. So then what happens: their journey together never ends, like the journey together to Emmaus. And the unity of the two spouses in Christ Jesus never ends. And so we have a beginning in time and an extension of life which never ends. This is why we say to the young person living in a changing world that Orthodox monasticism is the desert within, which is like the Kingdom of Heaven, where there is an unalterable stillness and a change without end, some deafening explosions which take place in silence. When the other person struggles, and waits patiently, and suddenly grace comes to him, and rest, which floods him and paralyses his members which are upon the earth, and he is filled with Paradise. And although this person is a simple, humble monk who is externally no different from anyone else, nevertheless he lives in Paradise. And although he does not travel the world or go on touristic excursions, nevertheless he is all the time on a journey. Then you have a sense of what it means that motionlessness is identified with movement. And this monk who has received this grace, who performs the simple task appointed to him and takes no notice of anything external — he is like many other humble people in the world. It may be a mother, a grandmother, a small child who has this grace. This is why in monasticism we say that it is not important whether your work is in the library or the refectory or somewhere else. What matters is this: as you work in this or that place with humility and love, have you received the grace of God which has turned everything into light? Because, you know, having a regime which is always the same gets on your nerves. In Orthodox monasticism, there is and is not a regime. And finally you have the sense that you are not saying a prayer, you become prayer. I once saw a monk going down from his cell to dig in the field. And I felt that his whole movement, the way he went down the terraces and dug, was prayer. Everything was within prayer: the digging and the earth and tools he was using. And he turns round and goes back to his cell and lights his lamp and says his prayers. And all this is within the state of grace, the repose of the age to come.

The same happens with what the saints say about prayer. At first prayer takes place by force, it takes place with prostrations. There is a struggle going on, as when the farmer ploughs the soil and sweats and gets tired. Finally the fruit comes as a reward for the farmer, and the operation of the prayer remains as a gift for the person who struggles in prayer. In the humble person, the breathing is spontaneously tied in with the prayer. And he breathes the prayer, "without any thought". Every breath is an inflammation, an injury to a wound he has within him. And the wound, as the "Anonymous Hesychast" says, becomes a spring.[10] And this spring, which flows from

[10] "The *pligi* becomes *pigi*" - the wordplay cannot be reproduced in English.

the inner wound of real love, nourishes the whole world. The fact that we are still alive, and breathe, and hope — perhaps this is due to these secret springs which nourish us from all sides. These springs come from the Mountain which is holy. The Mountain which is holy is the human being who is humble, who is contrite, who does not live for himself and has the grace of God. And you may find him on the Holy Mountain of Athos, or in Athens, or in this village.

Question: You have talked about humility in all aspects of a person's life, whether he is a monk or not; and I should like to ask you about pride, about the delicate distinction between humility and dignity, self-respect. Because very often we confuse these things. We try to appear humble — I find it confusing.

Fr. Vasileios: I think that someone who is humble is naturally dignified. Again, Abba Isaac says that "the humble and sagacious" do such and such. The humble person is "sagacious". The proud person is empty-headed. Don't we realise this? But I think that we are just groping after these things. Many people talk about humility, but I think that the great guide in the mystery of humility is Abba Isaac.

And he says: When I start to talk about humility I am afraid, because I am starting to talk about God Himself, because the Son and Word of God when He became man put on humility like a garment. And humility makes us Sons of God by grace, and humility brings the original grace of adoption, and afterwards every person is aware — and even the wild beasts too — that here they have the manifestation of God's compassion through the humble man. And everyone who is suffering and wounded (we all have our wound within us) receives consolation and strength. I think that what is needed is for us to live within the Church. Living within the Church, as we have said, with knowledge in its three degrees, which begins with the ascesis of virtue in a way that involves body and soul, and afterwards reaches that rest which is the foretaste of the life to come and of the Kingdom. So entering into the life of the Church is something that involves our body and our soul. Christ, as perfect God and perfect man, is the sanctification of souls and bodies. This is why I think it is important to live in the natural place. That means that, supposing I want to become a monk, I cannot but go the Holy Mountain. I have to go to the monastery, in other words. I cannot live in a flat in the middle of Athens. The Holy Mountain helps me with its services, its icons; I feel that when I am in my cell, in the garden, I am within the grace of the Mother of God, in her garden. Just as here it is a great blessing, and there could not be a better place for this meeting than under the protection of the Mother of God. There is this environment which helps us to achieve the meeting and the communication which is the aim of this congress. The mountain is a help, then.

...

Man is as God made him, and he wants not just

"goodness" but to attain to deification. And we are incapable even of goodness. Don't you know that we can't even be good? So then why are we talking about deification? Because we desire it, we seek it and God gives it to us as a free gift, when we are patient. And the saints who achieved this, achieved it also for our sake. They are a blessing for us, and we hope in their intercessions. So we should not be discouraged, and all problems will be solved through Orthodoxy. And we shall be saved through Orthodoxy. How? By each person carrying out his task properly. And I think that the little that is happening now with this meeting is a first step. Most of it will happen by itself, if we have ears to hear God's calling.

Question: You have said that on the Holy Mountain the monk feels at home, he is happy and so forth. But not all of us can go to the Holy Mountain — how is it possible to bring the Holy Mountain to the middle of Athens or the island of Lindos?

Fr. Vasileios: St. Basil the Great says somewhere that the true philosopher, whether he is in the desert or the teeming market-place, concentrates his mind in the monastery of his own self and occupies himself with prayer. I think that paradise and stillness are to be found not where there is no outward commotion — because I can go into a cave and be in the midst of Babylon — but we find stillness when we are where God sends us. Because if I have a strong constitution and a strong stomach which can take any kind of food, then I shall be in the desert within in the midst of Omonia Square, because I shall see everyone as my brothers. But I must not act in a way that is false; I should not go and do this sort of thing before I have acquired that strong stomach. A monk used to say: I don't know whether I am of more help to my brethren when I am in my hermitage, or whether I find greater stillness when I am living with them. That monk was free, and the point is that we are all called to achieve something like that. We all need that freedom — in order to live our monasticism as a true marriage with the grace of God, and our marriage as a true freedom which again is given us by the grace of God. This is why I think that in that place within, where the inner desert is a pulsating community of life — there there is no male or female, barbarian or Greek, central Athens or Holy Mountain, but a new creation where we are all gathered together and liberated by the Lord. And this is achieved through the life-bringing mortification which each of us can undergo insofar as he takes up his personal cross with patient endurance, and follows the Lord who suffered, leaving us an example (cf. 1 Peter 2:21).

Question: You have said a lot about humility today. I want to ask you: it seems to me that this humility is in conflict with the ethos of the world, and when one goes out into the world one will come into conflict with this ethos of humility. People say: they'll make mincemeat of you if you're like that. They'll destroy you. So what should we do? Why should we get destroyed? That is the first question. Secondly, you said at one point: the point is to be Orthodox, and then for each of us to carry out his task properly. But ultimately, what is the criterion for finding what is right and proper, what is true, what is orthodox, what is genuine? How will we know when we have found it?

Fr. Vasileios: On the first question: the point is that they should make mincemeat of us and destroy us, and the trouble is that they don't destroy us. You know that story from the sayings of the Desert Fathers, where a monk lived with a younger brother. And the younger brother had a relationship with someone else which the elder brother was not happy with. So he went and told his thoughts to another elder. And when the elder heard the story, he said, "You are still living"; the trouble is that you are still alive. If you were dead, you would not be bothered by anything. If you are three years in the grave, let's say, all your problems are solved. So, let's hope we do get punishments to destroy us. But I would say this, that the humility we are talking about, and which the saints are talking about, and which is a state of God's grace beyond virtue and is what makes a man "sagacious" — I think that this is the very grace which constitutes the whole institution of the Church[11] and constitutes the whole human being. And if we were constituted through humility by the grace of the

[11] Cf. Vespers for Pentecost.

Holy Spirit, then we should have no need of psychiatrists or of anything. One who is very humble is very weak and very strong.

The thing is that when we live within the Orthodox Church, we understand what is genuine, what is true. I want to say this: that what is true is full of stillness, it is calm. For something true, everything is a blessing. That is to say, if you praise it, it takes no notice; if you despise it, you are honouring it. Likewise with the good — it is a blessing for everyone. You see, the opposite, what is not genuine, lacks stillness. It is disturbed, changes disturb it and it transmits disturbance. Read one of the Fathers, Abba Isaac, and you will see how a sense of stillness floods your being. Approach someone who is in error, and you will see what disturbance it will cause you.

Our Church respects man. And it respects him in saying this: "If your heart is not at ease with someone, do not open your heart to him."

So we see that Orthodoxy puts us at our ease. No ideology, no revolution, no theory puts us at our ease. All these things have the form of truth, they have the coloration of truth, but they are not the whole truth. And we say that the whole truth is to be found in a place of stillness, and the whole truth sees everything as a blessing, both trials and blessings. And the whole truth is a blessing for everyone. And since it saves the whole person and each person, the whole truth puts us at our ease. This is why I think all this struggle takes place within us.

There is something else I want to say. When I talk

to Roman Catholics and we say Church, or theology, or liturgy, or monasticism, one has to be careful. We say that the Greek word *philotimo* has no equivalent in English or French.[12] Words for "theology", "Church" and "monasticism" do exist. But in reality these things do not exist, because the same terms have a different content. So when a Roman Catholic says "the Church", he means the Vatican. To me, that is not the Church. The Church for me is what happens after everything has been dissolved and then constituted by the grace of the Holy Spirit. And when they say "monasticism" and they mean various orders, one dedicated to a certain sort of work and another to another, I am not at ease with that. These are things that "dishonour a man". Here we do not think man exists in order to work, we do not want any work to be the purpose of his life. We want him to be saved; we want the words to burst from within him, "Glory to God that I am human!" And this "Glory to God" is work. If he builds or writes or paints icons, that has value, not because he has built something or painted an icon or written something, but because in his building and his icons and his books there is a different grace. And this grace is given to man free. This is what we are looking for. We say that what is true fears nothing; and we can also say this, that what is true comes about without effort. It is what happens at the third stage, in the state of

[12] This very characteristic Greek quality involves elements of self-respect, pride and "saving face".

freedom and rest. The Mother of God is she who bears Christ without effort. She never thought that she would become God's Mother. She was simply pure and humble, she effaced her own self and gave it to God. And God said to her: You will become the Mother who gives birth to God, and the Son and Word of God will be born according to the flesh from your womb. And it is she who effortlessly gave birth to God by the operation of the Holy Spirit who came upon her. Things that are true happen without effort. As the Lord says to us in the Gospel: "Consider the lilies of the field, how they grow; they toil not, neither do they spin." They do not tire themselves out, they do not weave, and not even Solomon in all his glory was clothed like one flower.

So this effortlessness is the truth, it is a blessing from God and it is offered to everyone. So what is true fears nothing, it sees everything as a blessing, it is not disturbed and does not transmit disturbance; it is a gift of the Holy Spirit and is given without effort; what is true and genuine is preserved not by appropriating it, by holding onto it so that no one can steal it, but by giving it freely to everyone. I am not going to repeat here what the Lord says, that whoever wants to save his life will lose it, and whoever loses it for the sake of the Lord and the Gospel, the joyful message, will save it: I am going to quote to you the popular saying, "Do what's good, and throw it on the shore." The best insurance if we want to save the "good" is to lose it, to throw it on the shore. And when everything is destroyed, the shore will bring out the good things which will clothe us in a different raiment so that we can present ourselves before the Lord. So you see that there is a different balance here, and after that man is not afraid of anything; everything is a blessing. And when someone hits me, I do not complain because he hits me when my time comes (and that too is important, when the time comes), but my complaint is that he hasn't destroyed me and ground me to dust. Because then the light which saves me will appear. You see in Solomos' poem "The Shark", how he says that when the shark devoured the young man,

"A light shone forth, and in that light the young man knew himself".

Poetry written in Greek, in the Orthodox world. This is why I say that here the teacher is taught something that saves the whole world. And we have a duty towards ourselves, the self which we must examine, the self which we must honour and respect, and save it through the Orthodox Church. And I think we have a duty towards all the children, all the young people. And for me, the young include the aged and the dead who are looking for something from those who have been baptised in the name of the Father and the Son and the Holy Spirit within the Orthodox Church. And especially from the Greeks.

Question: You have said that the thing is to live what God wills. In the modern world, faced with technology which makes us useless as human beings and science which boosts our conceit and makes us highly self-sufficient, faced with modern social and political and perhaps other structures which level us all out — how ought we to behave as people who are not happy with all this, as Christians let's say?

Fr. Vasileios: You heard the other day how the Bishop of Chania said that all these sciences are like lifting up a stone and finding a snail. Now you've found a snail, that's really something! You should be proud of finding the snail. So I think we must understand, living within the Orthodox Church, that all the progress in science is a matter of finding snails, and small snails at that. So it is of no value. Then here is something else: the things I am saying are all mixed up together. I do this on purpose, out of respect for you; if you want to respect me, pay no attention to me. And if you want to respect the things I say, throw them all in the wastepaper basket and take whatever's left over, if anything. Similarly from a meeting, or a book, or a talk, each person takes something very small. And that you should respect. That you should pay attention to. That will do its work and will help you to find for yourself the rhythm of your life, to speak your own language, and this is what is important. When you find the rhythm of your life, when you come to exist and when that "Glory to God" bursts from within you: then, having forgotten me and erased me from your mind, then you will remember me, then I too shall sense your "Glory to God!" This will be a refreshing dew for me and for all of us.

Question: I agree completely with what you say... But beyond that, shouldn't things perhaps be put into some sort of order, not so that we can find the snail — and while we are at it, let's go down 200 metres to find the snail, so we call in technology... Perhaps not all of us are made for stillness. It is possible that we may achieve it, and sometimes perhaps it is in rejecting that stillness that we find ourself; because often in the discussion here, and possibly also from what you are saying, someone might misconstrue it to mean that we are just seeking our own salvation.

Fr. Vasileios: I don't want things put into order. I want to give each person various bits and pieces, and I respect each person. The ordering is done by the make-up of each person. Everyone should throw out what he wants to and keep what he wants to. Even if he takes nothing, that is something. What is important is that he should move freely.

I go to a talk and I am enthused — it is debatable whether that is good or not. I go to another talk and I am pleased with it; whether it is good or not, I will see from what I take from it. I go to a third talk and get furious, and that is very good. Once I was listening to some sermons on the radio, and they made me furious from start to finish. Then on the question of technology; I think that the mind of the Orthodox Church is not afraid of technology and science, nor does it have crutches of that sort. But it lives in that state which the Kanon of the Akathist talks about: "The godly-minded children [in the furnace] did not worship creation, but the Creator." And when you worship the Creator, then you honour creation and use it in the proper way. And when you seek first the Kingdom of Heaven and its righteousness, then everything else that you need is added. And because it is added, it has a different grace and takes its proper place.

Then what you said about not all of us being made for stillness. We are all made for stillness, we want the depths of the desert and total stillness, because at the same time we are looking for social interaction and frenetic activity. We are all made for total stillness and for frenetic activity! Let's not say what is untrue, and everyone should move freely. When one is involved in frenetic activity within the Church, one enjoys total stillness; and when one is in stillness, one acts. It was the Apostle Paul who attained to the peace which passeth all understanding, while at the same time he was carrying the care of all the Churches.

...

Basically we all agree, and I just want a quarrel so that we can reach the one calm.

Question: I want to refer to someone who is always quarrelling, and that is the devil. I should like you to say something about him, because in the experience of the Holy Fathers and particularly monks he plays a major role. Since you have not referred to him at all, perhaps if you think it would be good you could say something to us about this lover of quarrels, the slanderer, who does not leave things as they genuinely are but creates various impressions, through which the true appears false and the false true.

Fr. Vasileios: I think that what you have said gives the answer well and clearly; but in what we have said, too, I think that the presence of the dark spirit is there invisibly, and he is trying to do one thing: to hide and not show himself, and when he does appear then he makes himself look ridiculous and he hides and shows up enormously, because he himself knows that he is ridiculous before the grace of God and before the person who has the grace of God. And I think it is clear that the whole spiritual struggle is a struggle for a discernment of spirits, that one has discernment and will have that discernment when one has passed through all this bodily ascesis, with the fasting and reading and prayer and patient endurance; when one gets to the point of receiving the grace of God, when one gets to the point of becoming "all eye", as the Saints say. On that point I want to say this: if we don't all reach the point of becoming "all eye", nevertheless living in the Church we understand this at some point. God "has not left any age without witness" (cf. Acts 14:17), and in the same way He has not left the soul of any man without witness. And supposing we do not have the experience that St. Paul or St. John the Theologian had, or other great Saints, still each of us has received the visitation of grace. So when one acquires this sense, one realises that a certain thing is from the evil one, and what is from the evil one, as the Apostle Paul says, is what brings you disturbance. And St. Isaac says that what is evil will bring you disturbance, arrogance, the feeling that you can look down on others; it will bring you a small and disordered mind. Finally, after this disturbance of the intellect and the soul, disturbance of the bodily members will follow and it will reach the point of a war of the flesh. If on the contrary something — some knowledge, some assurance, some state — comes from God, then it teaches you love, it makes you forgive everyone, and love everyone, and feel yourself to be lower than all creation; it makes this peace and ease go from your soul into the whole of your being, "into all my members, my reins and heart". And so after that one senses that this is of God — it gives one peace. Anything that gives me the feeling of being something more than other people, is of the evil one.

I remember a story one man told me... He had read *The Way of a Pilgrim*, he was saying the Jesus prayer and had made great progress in it, and when he said it his heart would pound. Then it would stop pounding. So he would run 100 metres to make it pound and then sit and say the prayer again, and his heart would pound. And when he got onto a 'bus he would say the prayer and look at the other people like so many ants — they don't know the prayer, they're like animals. —But better not to say the prayer than to look on other people as ants. As you see, there is something wrong there.

While by contrast someone else may say, I am dust

and ashes, I'm good for nothing and I know it, it's been proved and I give proof of it every day by the way I behave. On the other hand, if I have anything, it is a scandal of God's love. Abba Isaac says, God is not just — don't say that He is just, if He were just He would have burnt us up. God is all-good and He puts up with me. This is why I say that if something is of the evil one it will bring us disturbance, arrogance and permission from the devil not to forgive people, not to love some people. If someone has a thought from God, he loves everyone, he forgives everyone, with no question, and he feels that if there is something good, it is there by God's love and he himself does not deserve it.

Now, I think the devil is extremely clever and extremely stupid, extremely large and extremely small; that is why the Fathers call him an "ant-lion". If we feed him, we make him into a lion; if we have the grace of God, he becomes an ant and ridiculous. On the other hand, I think the devil has two cassettes — not several cassettes, just two. He puts one on for you. You say, I've heard it. Listen to it again, then, he says — listen to the other side. I've heard the other side as well. Well then, the other side again. I've heard it. No, he says; you know, it's something really amazing. Afterwards the devil sends you a parcel, very beautifully wrapped, with red ribbon and a gold bow. I don't want it, you say. — But it's amazing. — I know what's in it and I don't want it. That's why I would say this: just as it is, with the red ribbon and the gold bow, it should be thrown out of the window.

And we should each get on with our business. Then things are simplified. If we start discussions, what with the cassette and the gifts, we waste our time, we make ourselves miserable and the devil has accomplished his task. The other thing: what he tries to do is to hide; he wants us to find theology in the devil's cassette and think there is something to eat in the devil's gifts. That is why the Fathers say that our whole effort is to reach the point and make that distinction between spirits: this is from the devil and I'm throwing it away; this is from the grace of God and I accept it; something else comes from the make-up of the human being,

It does not mean that if I'm sluggish I am humble; it does not mean that if I am irritable, I have the zeal of the prophet Elijah — I'm just irritable. Living within the Church, doing what we are commanded, doing what we should and enduring patiently, above all, if we have the honour of being visited by trials, then the grace of God will surely come and will teach us what cannot be taught. And then we shall understand what is the grace of God and what is the devil, that figure of fun who constantly tries to slander the love and power of God.

Question: I should like to express three thoughts: not that I personally accept them or reject them, but they are in a way stumbling blocks for me and perhaps also for everyone. Firstly, all that you have said touches me very deeply; but because I am not able to live these things to the extent that I should, in a way they do not touch me. They are close to me, and they are far away from me. For instance, what you say about being separated from everything in order to be united with everything — I have difficulty grasping that even just intellectually. Secondly, the question of human reasoning... for instance when we talk about human knowledge. My thinking is that if you have human knowledge and you become holy, that is something. If you know foreign languages and you become holy, that too is something. And again the fact that you are here talking to us, you are not at this moment somewhere far away — even on the Holy Mountain — that too is something: something tangible, something real. And the third thing, I think, is focused on the Gospel of the Last Judgement. In this Gospel we read that the ultimate criterion for our salvation or condemnation is nothing other than a practical expression of love. It says nothing to us about prayer or stillness, or about monasticism; it doesn't even talk about a relationship with God. It simply talks about helping man. I should like you to comment on these three difficulties.

Fr. Vasileios: I can't live these things, they are far away and close by. I think that is always the way it is. A poet says, I have written this poem. And usually a real poet is like a monk. Abba Isaac says somewhere that there was a monk who covered the wall of his cell with sayings. And when a visitor came in and asked him, what's all this, he said: these are things I write down at the time when grace visits me. And when grace leaves me, I read them and draw strength from them. So this poet says — I wrote this poem at a moment when I felt something. If at some time someone else experiences something similar, he will find it — he will find the same frequency. I think that what we have said (first of all, I don't know whether it is because I am just like that or because I have said these things a thousand times) — it all seems to me very simple. A second point, I feel at ease with these things. Thirdly, they are old and modern; and fourthly, they are not my own bright ideas, they are within the Church. So then we say these things, and I have told you how I want you to receive them. I want you to hear them and to respect yourselves. And to leave yourselves in peace. It is your own self that will put things into order and classify them. There are sieves inside us which can judge: I will throw this away or I will keep this. Throw away what you want to and keep what you want to. As we said about what is true, it is far away and nearby. There are certain things which recede when we approach them, and when we move away from them they approach us. Isn't that so? As for how one will sense this, and when: the time will come and one will sense it. We'll leave it at that. But these things that I am saying to you — do you think they all correspond to my own state? I can only say this: I love them, and that is why I say them. And perhaps someone else will embody them better and take them further.

As to human knowledge, I want to say this. It is good for each person to follow his path in Christ Jesus and to do his own appointed task: this one in the garden, another in the library, another in science, another in art. If we take this to the end, somewhere we shall all be united. In a place that is warm and spacious. Spacious without being chaotic, and warm without stifling us and having that suffocating self-preservation which, as someone said, is just about taking over. At some point "action comes to an end", the senses cease to function and one goes beyond knowledge and sense perception and freedom, and advances into a different state. Now, the thing is that since it is possible for man, for human nature, to get there, and we have that breath of God within us, this gives us a great consolation. Do you feel at ease with knowledge and science? Go on with them, then; only go on with them to the end. And at the end we shall all meet, and we shall all be set free. I will use this image: When an aeroplane is on the runway for take-off, it is using its wheels. When it gains speed, it is using its wheels. When it gains still more speed, it finds another means of support; it is in the air. At that point the wheels are not needed, they just get in the way. But whereas the runway will end and lead into the sea or the rocks, the plane does not crash into the sea or the rocks. It has gone off somewhere else. Before the runaway ends, it has found a different means of support and so it doesn't have a crash. Before this life ends, man has to find a different means of support. And by the time death comes, he no longer treads this earth. He treads somewhere else. And I think that one can get onto the runway for takeoff starting from science, or art, or whatever else one wants. The point is that he is able to find a different means of support. And that at some point he can see the terror of death and see the earth like a tiny dot, while he himself is going forward by the grace of God. And because this exists in the Orthodox Church, this is why we say that it is good for all the world. Whereas I listen to some theories or "theologies" which are like airports with no runway for takeoff. These are the things which restrict man and abuse the aeroplane. The aeroplane has to take off — it is not a push-cart you can use to sell tomatoes from in the market. It has a different destiny. And man too has a different destiny. He can start where he likes. He can start from freedom, so that by the grace of God he will be released even from his freedom.

As for the practical expression of love — again, we can say that if someone feels like giving this poor man a piece of bread — even though there are not the poor people today that there were in the '40s and '50s... But I think that the greatest help and the greatest expression of love that we have to give to everyone is to sanctify our own vessel. This is why when someone repents, he becomes a sign of hope for the whole world. "There is joy in heaven over one sinner who repents." You have seen how a forest is destroyed in South America, and oxygen is destroyed throughout the world. If one person repents, if one person receives the grace of God, he supplies the oxygen of life and hope to the whole world. I may give my aid by giving someone a piece of bread or a book; someone else, without doing anything, just being somewhere, sends forth a radiance which gives hope to the whole world. So each person should of course show his love. And you know the other thing that Abba Isaac says, that God is nothing but love, and the last judgement will be carried out by love; the point is for us to accept that love as a blessing and not as a curse. And someone was saying: who will be able to love the person who has become so twisted that he experiences love as hell, and is unable to love? And someone used to say that in paradise, God will say to everyone, "Come into paradise." "What happens there?", they will ask. "There is praise of God, there is a climate of love, of interpenetration." So this person says, "No way, that's hell — I'm going." And that is the way one goes to hell, which is the lack of love. So in one way or another, all our life is a matter of dependence on love. But since you say I talk in paradoxes, I want to tell you this:

In Cyprus once, we went to Kyperounta for Vespers. And the old priest there, one of those uneducated village priests, received us with absolute tenderness without paying any attention to us, because there was not the slightest sentimentality in his nature. While someone else might show me love, and I want to say, can't you just leave me alone. But with this man I felt that he radiated a warm love by his total contempt. This is something orthodox and beautiful. When someone moves freely, he is genuine and everything around him becomes good.

Question: I want to pause for a moment on humility. This word "humility" shocks me somehow. It is all very well for monks... but for those of us who live in the world, I'm afraid there is a danger that in the name of some sort of humility — we are the lamp, and so forth — we might stop being involved in various areas of society. I should like you to tell us, is it possible to have that social involvement while preserving humility?

Fr. Vasileios: Someone once said to me: What with the things you say and all this freedom, don't you think the young might go overboard? Well — I can't say that I allow freedom. One needs to be bound *voluntarily*. If one is not bound voluntarily, then it's no good, it is not worth the trouble. Now on the subject of humility and obedience, this can be abused; I could say to a monk, be obedient to me. But the point is not that he should be obedient to me. The point is to help him to be obedient to the will of God. And this obedience to the will of God is like the airliner using its wheels in order to take off — it is a matter of getting onto the right road which will lead you to freedom. And the other person wants freedom. So by obedience to the will of God, he is set free. One should take it is this sense. So the Orthodox monastery is put together in disintegrating; and when you give everyone else freedom in order for them to obey the will of God, in this way it acquires a different grace and a different dimension. And so it is not our house or our club, but a community whose bounds are those of the Church, which means those of the whole world. And you have to give the other person the possibility of making mistakes so that he can be corrected. Otherwise, he is not going to be corrected. If you want to make other people be obedient or humble by squirting an aerosol at them to stun them, then you will indeed have peace and quiet, but you will have a row of zombies in front of you. But if you want to let each person find his own way, to let him repent, then it will be a headache for both you and him, but that headache will lead both of you to the real peace and grace because in the end, everything will happen of its own accord. And we are "gathered together by the Lord", as Isaiah says somewhere,[13] those who are scattered shall not stray, but shall be gathered together by the Lord. You see that the scattering has the grace of an assembly, and the assembly has the spaciousness of freedom; because men will be gathered together by the Lord. So this is how obedience and humility come about, and it is a great gift which one will savour once one understands it. As the funeral service says, "May I also find the way through repentance"; that is a great gift. There are some who very easily find the grace of the humility which exalts, and so they make progress. Others do not find it and do not make progress. But again, I would say that the Orthodox Church is everything, and that is where we shall be taught humility and obedience properly. Not outside.

---

[13] Cf. Isaiah 35.

Don't give obedience to me, or to someone else. I as an elder or someone else as a spiritual father needs to lead the other person to Christ and the Mother of God, to the Church; not to myself, or my party, or my viewpoint. First of all, I do not have confidence in myself. But I do have confidence in the Altar to which I lead the monk. And then the priest asks, "Why have you come here, brother?" (Falling before the Holy Altar and this holy community.) He falls before the Holy Altar and the Holy Community, and so I am at peace. And he comes forward in all freedom.

As for social involvement: as we have said, you start from the Church and from the ultimate desire, which is that man should not die, and from there on each person should follow his own path. And if that has to go through social involvement, or he thinks it does, then he should get involved in social areas. Everything that we say or do judges us, I think. And if we have a good disposition, we shall keep on advancing further, and we shall reach that place where we are all united and set free.

Question: Someone who lives and moves in the modern world — can he carry on mental prayer and reach the stage you mentioned earlier in which the prayer is united to one's breathing? Is this possible?

Fr. Vasileios: First of all, I am allergic to the phrase "the modern world". Secondly: what is traditional in Orthodoxy is modern, and also belongs to the future. Prayer endures in stillness and in commotion. It gives meaning to both the stillness and the commotion. If someone told me that I should say the Our Father and Psalm 50, or other Psalms (the ancient monks in Nitria usually learnt the Psalter by heart), that is harder in the "bus or amidst crowds." But it is easier to say the one-sentence prayer "Lord Jesus Christ, Son of God, have mercy on me a sinner." I feel that You, Jesus, whom I don't know, insofar as I do know You (I know You beyond knowledge) — You are who You are, You are the mighty One. I am weak, I am lost, I am a sinner. I ask Your mercy. "Lord Jesus Christ, Son of God, have mercy on me a sinner." This is a one-sentence prayer. And Gregory of Nyssa says that it is like the manna in the wilderness which is a food of one kind but also of great variety. So this traditional prayer is also more modern, because it can keep us company everywhere and all the time. They often say that it requires a teacher. The teacher is humility. We spoke before about the man who saw other people as ants. But when I am aware that I am weak and I feel the need to seek God's mercy, then it will come when it comes. And then it will join itself to my breathing spontaneously. And if something like that happens (as the Fathers say, I may not be saying the prayer but still have the operation of the prayer within me) I must not be proud of it, because that means I am lost. And another thing: does it ever enter our heads to be proud of breathing? Well, in rather the same way, as the body needs oxygen to refresh the blood, so our spiritual organism needs this spiritual oxygen. And I think that if humility is there, all the commotions and troubles will help us to make good progress.

Question: I want to pause on the title of your talk, "Monasticism and the new realities of life". I should like to know what stance monasticism takes, firstly, towards the new technological realities of our time; and more specifically, you referred to a new well and a fridge... is that from necessity, or the result of a certain stance towards new technological realities, and if so what is that stance? And secondly, what is the stance of monasticism towards the new ethical and social realities of our time? Even more specifically, I think that perhaps the most important reality of our time is the new position of women... What is the stance of monasticism and, if you like, of the Holy Mountain, because as we know women are not allowed onto the Mountain?

Fr. Vasileios: First of all, good for you, that as a man you are asking about women. As to technology, I think that the answer should have been given more or less — that you should have picked it up for yourself. We say that one should not be dominated by technology. There is a struggle going on not to be dominated, but to use things in a right way, which is eucharistic and gives glory to God. And like you, all of us are going through a trial; monasticism is, and it is being judged, and Athonite monasticism much more so because right from the beginning things were rather more ascetic and more difficult on the

Holy Mountain compared with monasteries outside. So at the time when it would have been possible to open up roads and have cars, this was not done. Now there are some roads from Daphni to Karyes and Iveron, and then some logging roads. In the old days there were many monks who were labourers. There were many visiting monks who regarded it as a blessing to come and help out. The people who came as pilgrims came under difficult conditions. Now there is a ferry and it brings in thousands. The people who come to the Holy Mountain now are not manual labourers. Then large numbers gather and you have to feed them and find them somewhere to sleep and wash the sheets, the monks are few, they haven't the physical endurance of the monks in the old days, so something has to be done. And I think the problems are resolved because you realise that man is himself created in the image of God, and he should have some rest. Again, each one of us is a visitor to the Mountain, and we all have the same rights. If I stay there 30 or 40 years and someone else stays there one day, it makes no difference. He has the same rights; the Holy Mountain is his home. And that man who is there for one day may be more of an Athonite than I who have stayed for 40 years. So one attempts not to destroy the atmosphere of the Mountain, and at the same time to use all these technological means in the right way. We are currently building a new wing, and first of all you should know that there is an Athonite monastic flavour in material things too. That is to say, when you go into a hospital you sense that it is a hospital — or a super market, or a house like this — or you sense when you are going into an Athonite monastery. This flavour has to be preserved. And you need to be architect, archaeologist and monk — you must have a sense for these things. Material things are directly related to spiritual things. An Athonite church shows love for mankind in a physical way: it has thick walls, and keeps you warm in winter and cool in summer. When you go in you sense a spiritual fragrance from the incense, the olive oil in the lamps and the pure beeswax. It has light if you want it, and dark side-chapels. You can stand up or sit down. The services takes place during the day or at night. There are the vigils where at some points the appointed monk lights the lamps, and at other points he puts them out. All these things, these simple, formal, material things, are of great significance for spiritual life. And as it is in the church, so it is in the whole organisation of the monastery... today we have to use the culture of technology, but we do so with great care. Not that the culture of technology is bad in itself, but what is of paramount importance is the way it is used. Again, modern media judge us, even in building. Things like reinforced concrete. Concrete is not evil. The old-fashioned materials, brick, stone and wood, used by people who were spiritually balanced, are a help to us today. If we had those materials — stone, brick, wood, plaster — it would be much easier to make fewer mistakes. When we have cement and iron, we have to be much more careful. So much for technology.

As to the position of women, that is a whole vast

subject. I can say — you should be more or less used to the way I talk — that the weak sex is the strong one; for as Paul says, when I am weak, then am I strong and powerful. Woman is respected, given ultimate respect and flourishes and shines through the person of the Mother of God, who was revealed as "More honourable that the cherubim and glorious incomparably more then the seraphim" — when she lives within the Orthodox Church. Outside the Orthodox Church, when she instigates various movements, it is not that human nature is "dishonoured", as Abba Isaac says; it is utterly degraded. But to understand this is again something great and sacred.

Question: If one is a teacher, or a godparent, or a brother or most of all a parent, how can one give a child that humility we were talking about earlier, the solid food of Orthodox faith?

Fr. Vasileios: We can take the children to play somewhere that is near the Church. They should have proper icons, without our giving them explanations of the theology of the icon. There should be the proper sort of singing in church; and then if we have understood that it is humility that exalts us, that life-giving mortification makes us partakers of eternal life, we don't need to talk to them in these terms — we just need to love them. By the way we talk to them and laugh with them, we convey to them that which is incomprehensible, which is beyond speech and perception.

Question: ... How does the Holy Mountain participate — how should it participate — in the expression of truth through the Church... and in the expression of truth through the various problems of the Church? And secondly: I am thinking what a difference there is in the exercise of humility for someone who lives in the world, and for a monastic. The monastic exercises humility voluntarily — he himself humbles himself. He does not have external irritations — or if he does, they will be from some spiritual person who, he knows, has his interest at heart. Whereas in the world, we often find that other people humiliate us, and we have to exercise our humility in the face of abuse and blasphemies and insults. In other words, we see how much more difficult it is, and how much more strength it takes, to train oneself in humility in the world... It is one thing to obey an elder whom you regard as a spiritual person and who you know is doing it for your good, and quite another to act with humility towards someone who abuses you and insults you, without your knowing whether that will affect your professional career and your family and your life in general.

Fr. Vasileios: ... You wonder whether the Mountain should not provide some point of reference in the Church's problems. But I can say that it does provide such a point of reference by its existence. What was said earlier about technology bears some relation to this. The spiritual and cultural tradition of the Mountain in on a very high level. If we carry on this way of living as we have received it, then we are intervening — often while absent, but present in another way — in the Church's problems. I think that monasticism is a help in that way. Just as a Saint helps who is invisible, who has fallen asleep but is seen invisible, who manifests himself.

On the subject of humility: to begin with, what Abba Isaac says about "the other means that dishonour man" — Isaac, and all the Saints, talk about man. Abba Isaac advises the monk, saying: "Live in a dwelling unseen by men, and unlike the dwellings of men." He himself lived in the desert. So the monk who lives in a cenobitic monastery reads Abba Isaac and himself has to translate this, because the setting of Isaac's life was the inner desert. But despite all this, he lays the foundations of Orthodox anthropology, or if you like just of anthropology. I feel that what is important is that we are human beings, not whether we are monks or non-monks. Every humiliation or humiliating action on the part of someone else, towards the person who has understood what man's nobility is, is something that honours him, glorifies him and nurtures him. The wind may sweep down on the sea like a demonic blast with the intention of sinking a ship. And then a skilled captain hoists his sail the way he wants it and at the angle he wants it, and it takes him soundlessly, without... effort, to the island he wants to go to, and he says to the wind, to the demon, I'm grateful to you, because otherwise I would have worn myself out rowing. So those who want to harm us and humiliate us, do us good. We just have to take a small dose of the Kingdom of Heaven, of the mystical grace which is offered by the Church and by our Saints. Haven't we said that what is true and genuine is that which rejoices in everything, and does not get upset over anyone, and has no complaints about anything?

- Epilogue -

There is no epilogue; we should leave the subject open. However small your boat is, you cannot direct its course by the island it is going past, or by a cloud blown by the wind; even the smallest of boats is orientated by the Pole Star, which remains fixed and indicates the centre of the world. Thus we all stand in need of that light of Christ which illumines all, and of the Saints who are the heavenly bodies which guide us. So all of us, however small we may be, need that light on high. The other thing is this: that one goes through many trials, and the prayer for the tonsuring of a monk talks about the sorrows of the gladdening life in God. Monastic life is good because it is a great ordeal. And the thing is that these ordeals and difficulties reveal within you something that does not torment, but always consoles. After the clouds, whatever they may be, the sun comes out again. And you feel like this: you enter into the regime of life, and you get on well and you are nurtured. A difficulty comes along; it might be a fire, or some other disaster which throws your regime into disarray. And if you have found the secret, the regime may be upside down but your stillness is not perturbed. If your stillness is perturbed because your regime is upside down, this means that you lack endurance. And so when you see that everything is in disarray but stillness remains, then you feel that after death, too, your body will turn to dust and yet your soul will live. Something else: there is something that leaves a deep mark on us, what we say about receiving the grace of God through humility and patient endurance. A monk may receive this. But when I see the thief going into paradise first and the disciples staying outside — at that moment one of them is swearing that "I don't know Him", another is betraying Him. And you think, it is not possible here to put things into a neat order. There is something stable, and something which turns everything upside down. And the stable element is that God loves us, and that each of us is the image of God, and that if I have committed crimes, those crimes are "marks", as it says in the funeral service: "I am an image of Thine ineffable glory, though I bear the marks of transgressions." It calls my crimes "marks". And what happens? The greatest thing is the love of God and His image hidden within us. May He grant us in the moments of difficulty to say in repentance, "Remember me, O Lord", so that His love may conquer and we may attain the promised good things which have not entered into the heart of man, and which the Lord who wills that all should be saved has prepared, as Father and Almighty. Amen.